YOU GREW TALLER THAN THE PALM

Poems Of The Black African Struggle

Series One

IKECHI AKURUNWA

Books by Ikechi Akurunwa

Poetry

In the Palm of her hand
You Grew Taller Than the Palm
Morning Will Surely Come

Non-Fiction

The Cardinal Laws of Freedom
Self-Examination: The Path to Being Free & Staying Free

Copyright @ 2021 by Ikechi Akurunwa

All rights reserved. No part of this book may be reproduced or transmitted in any form without the written permission of the author or publisher.

Book Express Publishing House books may be ordered through booksellers or www.goexpresspublishing.com

ISBN: 978-0-9729525-0-7 (Paperback)
ISBN: 978-1-955495-00-4 (Hardback)
ISBN: 978-0-9729525-4-5 (ebook)

First Printing
Printed in the United States of America
Print information available on the last page.
Library of Congress Control Number: 2021935880 (Paperback)
Library of Congress Control Number: 2021937719 (Hardback)

BOOK EXPRESS PUBLISHING HOUSE
Atlanta, Georgia
www.goexpressbulishing.com

DEDICATION

*To every African
dreaming of a free Africa.*

Contents

PROLOGUE ix

ONE 1

   Flashbacks of Racism 3

   The Pen 4

   Mpho's Tale of Apartheid 5

   Apartheid 9

   Oh, England 11

   The West 13

   Karabou's Memories of Apartheid 15

   Amadi's Lamentation Over Colonialism 17

   Opinions and Prejudices 20

   A Different Battle 23

   You Grew Taller Than the Palm 25

TWO 29

   I Have Seen So Much 31

   Wooden Treasure 34

   A Forgotten People 38

   Not Enough Time 42

   If You Are Looking for Me 44

   Come with Me 47

   All Is Not Well 50

   A Strong Resolve 52

    The Dancing Feather 54

    Oh, Come Rain 57

THREE **61**

    What Troubles Me 63

    Letter to the Black African President 66

    Poor Historian 70

    Devoured Inheritance 72

    Heart Cry from the Slum 74

    How Did You Forget? 76

    This Land 80

    Against All Odds 82

FOUR **85**

    Self-Destruction 87

    Dangerous Trend 89

    The African Heart 92

    Bundles of Nothing 95

    Invitation 97

    Little by Little 99

    My Afro-Caribbean Brothers and Sisters 101

    I Still Believe 103

    Sound the Alarm 106

PROLOGUE

You Grew Taller Than the Palm is intended to tell Africa's story from a poetic viewpoint. Its focus is not on any individual African person or country; rather, this poetry draws the curtain for the reader to see the face of Africans forging through the wild winds of colonialism, tyranny, and self-inflicted injuries. It unveils the face of the African struggle, the face of those who are clawed to death in the journey, and those who daily claw their way through the dark to rise to the top.

You Grew Taller Than the Palm is not only the story of Black Africa. It throws a lot of light on the faces that created the colonial African state and the cruel footprints they left behind, as well as the faces of Africans who have continued where the West left off.

Ikechi Akurunwa

You Grew Taller Than The Palm

You Grew Taller Than The Palm

ONE

Africa, the flame kindled
by your colonial masters
is still burning.

Ikechi Akurunwa

Flashbacks of Racism

Some days, I follow the silent
footsteps of my thoughts
to places I don't want to remember,
places they looked at me and laughed,
places they told me, "You don't belong here."

Some days, I follow the lingering memories
of my past or the shadows of my old footprints
to places that scarred my soul,
places they told me, "You are not one of us."
places they told me, "Go back to your slum."

Some days, I follow the trail
of my blood to places I escaped death,
to places I was shaken to my bones,
places I was chased with a club,
and told, "You are not welcome here."

Some days, I follow the trail
of my tears to the presence of God.
And there, I wholeheartedly thank Him
that my faith does not lie solely
in the hands of mortal men.

Ikechi Akurunwa

The Pen

The pen in my hand is dancing
with the flickering flame
of the African lamp

daily pushing against
the unrelenting darkness
of imperialism,

hoping that one day
it will teach the West how to dance
from the heart and not from the lips.

Mpho's Tale of Apartheid

Don't tell me it's wrong to ask
why they wanted us to be their slaves
in our own land, or why
they drew a line on the sand
we were not allowed to cross,
villains with burning secrets
tucked behind fake smiles.

Don't tell me it's wrong to ask
why they drummed into our ears
with tongues like stonecutting blades,
that nothing good
can come from Africans
while forcefully
stripping our lands from our hands.

Don't tell me it's wrong to ask
why everything about us
stirred up rage in their hearts,
or why they always stared
at us condescendingly,
with blank eyes buried in hollow sockets,
and veins, disheveled like fibrous roots,
by the hate surging through them.

Ikechi Akurunwa

I asked why then, and I ask why now,
because after so many years
of the hellish Apartheid regime,
the monstrous shadows
of white racist police officers
shooting South Africans without cause
still follow me around.
Even when I am alone,
I sometimes find myself
running from imaginary shadows
of white men with guns.

I still ask why because their harsh
and cruel words that built a nest in my soul
still echo in my ears every day.
Even when it rains,
I still hear them in the rain.
Even when it thunders,
I still hear them in the thunder.
Even in the silent hours of the day,
I still hear them screaming in our ears
with anger and hatred laced
around their faces like a rim of fire.

Oh, how grateful I will be the day
my brain will be rid of the memory
of how our faces were rubbed
with the despicable ashes of shame,
day after day.

You Grew Taller Than The Palm

They make my head heavy like lead.
The memory of the Pass laws,
Group Areas Acts, Influx Control laws,
and all the other laws
designed to torment,
marginalize,
and incarcerate us
in their lynching jails.

Oh painful wounds I may never forget.
The tears and anguish of the wives
and children of black miners
who died in the mines trying
to scrape all the gold from the belly
of South African soil, so the white populace
could live luxuriantly in their white heavens.

Oh unfathomable anguish.
The memory of all the black prisoners
regularly beaten and tortured,
and sometimes starved and hanged
on miserable trees, then buried
in contemptible graves.

And the horrid sights of all those black
political activists, hanged with their belts
or clothes or blankets, but labeled
suicides by white police.

Ikechi Akurunwa

How can I ever forget
all these humiliations,
all these tortures,
all these assaults,
all these abuses
meted out to us in our own land,
day after day, night after night,
like we were animals
who don't deserve to live?

How can I ever forget all that?
Maybe I will someday
if someone would tell me
why they did all that to us?

Why did they do that to us?

Why?

Apartheid

At the time when the moon still ripened
in the African sky
like polished gold
and darkness
had nowhere to hide,
a flag sprung up in the air,
bearing a white flame.

It was Apartheid.
A red and painful boil
that suddenly sprouted
on the skin
of South Africa.

By day it grew.
By night it grew.
It grew until it burst with rage,
spitting its racial flames all over the land,
and setting the land of South Africa
into a deadly
conflagration.

It was a cruel fire that took the lives
of many innocent South Africans.
Those who were not killed

were gruesomely tortured
and stripped of their dignity
with guns and blunt force
until their minds became a powder keg
of anguish and resentment.

Ironically, no matter how hard
the cruel invaders and other proponents
of white supremacy tried,
the land of South Africa never whitened
as fast as they wanted it
before the exhausted filaments
of Apartheid began to burn out.

But, even when the flame
of Apartheid
finally died,
the boil never healed. It only
receded under the skin of the land
from where till this day,
it still rears its contemptuous head,
from time to time.

Oh, England

We will never forget you, England.
Not with your twisted lips still reciting
the same old deceptive sermons.

Not with our dawn still forced
to fly your imperial flag—
that symbol of conquest,
that specter of shame,
that banner of humiliation,
with edges tainted with our blood—
which you proudly raise up and down
its iron lady pole
every day
to remind us that the old
blood-stained leash of slavery
in your hands is unbreakable.

Oh, we will never forget you, England.
Not with your cold laughter,
not with your cold face,
not with your cold hands,
not with your cold heart,
not with your cold swords,

or your cruel hangmen—

Ikechi Akurunwa

blood-thirsty zealots
still doing your bidding,
constantly disrupting
the fragile peace in our land.

Oh England, England.
We will never forget you.
Not with all
you've put us through.

The West

Before any more of your antics,
imposing rosary,
or hypocritical pious chants,
show me your true face,
since all I have seen is your back.

Before my face is covered again
by your fox fur
and my eyes blinded
by the glare of your mask,
tell me, when will your yea be yea
and your nay be nay?

Since you invaded Africa,
our rivers and the rivers of the world
have not ceased to gloat
about how you filled them
with the bloated bellies
of African children
that fell to your sword,

children you buried in unholy graves
without uttering a single prayer
for their innocent souls.

Ikechi Akurunwa

Before you feed me
another old fable,
or fill my ears with another old fairytale,
show me your true face,
for all I have seen
is your back.

You Grew Taller Than The Palm

Karabou's Memories of Apartheid

Until the air was filled with the smell
of gunpowder and the sound
of repeated gun blasts
as they sought to establish
their cruel dominance over our land,
we did not know the smiling faces from Europe
that we welcomed on our shores with open arms,
were not angels.

We didn't know that soon
the bones of everyone they touched
would be broken by the rod of subjugation,
the lands of everyone they visited
would be snatched by the forceful fist of greed,
the cloths of everyone they embraced
would be burned by the fire of hate.

They were as sharp as their swords,
as cold as their words.
And because we said no as they tried
to force their unholy laws on us,
they imprisoned Nelson Mandela,
Denis Goldberg, and others
who rose to defend our land.

They were as gutty as their guns,
as gusty as the wind.
And because they wouldn't take no
for an answer as they sought to turn us
into dispensable and disposable
human commodities,
they killed Steve Biko,
Solomon Mahlangu,
Neil Aggett, Ashley Kriel,
and others who stood up for our rights.

But as the omnivorous mouth
of apartheid widened
and their oppressive hands pounded
more and more furiously on our doors,
we rose up daily, against all odds,
and cheered those who defended our land,

keeping the fire of freedom
burning in our hearts
until the day our undying spirit outlived
the era of Apartheid in South Africa.

Amadi's Lamentation Over Colonialism

Brother, where have you been?
Have you not seen the wild wind
from England torching our land
with flames that seem to levitate in the air
like an unfolding bad omen,
like the head of an angry cobra,
like an unraveling day of sorrow?

I think this deserves your attention,
and the attention of every indolent ear.

Since those strangers with Victorian top hats
came and infested our leaders with greed,
the wild wind of subjugation has not ceased.
It has spread its scourge all over the land,
bestowing to our beguiled leaders
new cogs in the cogwheel of repression,
and filling their mouths with profanity
that they now spew in our faces,
like the blinding dust of the Sahara.

Today, our land is riddled with sores
that our leaders have refused to tend to.
Rather, with their polished European shoes
they have scuffed our old landmarks so deep

Ikechi Akurunwa

they have exposed worms to hungry birds,
and now our greedy politicians
and men with long reaching arms
are in a feeding frenzy.

Brother, are you not worried?
Everything is slowly dying.
Our people are dying,
our dreams are dying,
our farms and vegetation are dying.
Even the Lala palms, the mahoganies,
the baobabs, and the iroko trees
that made our land beautiful,
have been stripped bare
by the persistent hands
of this strange wind.

I am worried by our withering land.
I am worried by the many hands
beating the drum of sorrow
and feeding the fear in my heart.

Every day, the mouths
of our invaders widen,
and their claws grow sharper.

Even our children have abandoned
their playgrounds in fear.
Their trembling mouths no longer sing.

Their paralyzed feet no longer dance,
neither can their shaking hands hold
or cuddle their toys.

We have become a people
in perpetual bondage,
a people forced to silently watch
as our mantles fall,
as our crowns fall,
as our thrones fall,
as our kingdoms fall,
and as our countries fall,
one by one
under the oppressive hands
of colonialism.

Brother, we have become a people
in perpetual bondage,
with no reprieve in sight.

Ikechi Akurunwa

Opinions and Prejudices

With age and time racing ahead of me,
with seas and waves swelling around me,
with winds and clouds daily frowning at me,
I have no greater desire at dawn
than to shut out the noise from the lips
of mongers howling in my ears
to make my burden heavier.

Why is the world so obsessed that my neck
has not been adorned with a papal rosary?
Why is she so hysteric that my hands
have not, for once, borne an Olympic medal,
or that my head has not yet worn
the crown of a famous poet?

I have made up my mind that there is no need
to wallow in the whirlpool of endless opinions
and prejudices of friends, or foes,
or lose sleep over the sprawling sand
that constantly makes my footprints
look like the tracks of a mysterious beast,
or a drunk who cannot find his way home.

I no longer live my life
looking for the soft pillows

of people's kind opinions and affirmations
on which to lay my head.

I have no more desire to explain myself to souls
looking to nourish their empty hearts
with the dirge from the whispering lips
of idle minds burning with envy.

I no longer have the appetite to live my life
venerating the tongues of strangers
twisted by pride and prejudice,
wolves from whose hands
words have been shot like arrows
into the hearts of innocent Africans.
Villains from whose hands the water
of desolation has poured for centuries
on the wounds of vulnerable Africans,
leaving their souls with deep scars.

Friend, life has taught me that prejudice
is nothing but an empty net
cast in the air.
As long as you ignore it,
it will plunge to the ground
and rot away with time.

And I have come to the realization
that people's opinions are nothing
but grains of sand

Ikechi Akurunwa

tossed into the vast air.
As long as you leave them alone,
their lifeless bodies will fall to the ground
and quickly disappear
in the gaping mouth of the sand.

A Different Battle

I am not one of those gifted
with the grey matter of musicians
who play instruments with closed eyes,

or one of those with the brain
of a cleric who has memorized
every verse of the Pentateuch,

or one of those with the wits
of a sage whose philosophical thoughts
have shaped and framed the minds
of great thinkers.

But I know enough
to figure out that in life
you cannot fight alone
the venoms of hatred
hidden in a dark heart.

That's why when the world
casts her usual aspersions on me
because of my color,
or throws another layer of shrouding cloth
over the breathing body of Africa
to exclude her from the living,

Ikechi Akurunwa

I seize the opportunity
to affirm and reaffirm who I am
to myself and my Creator.

Probably, they don't know
in whose image I was made,
or the coming dawn of Africa
that I see.

Even as the world tries hard every day
to define and redefine Africa,
or to label and relabel me,
I shrug off from my shoulders
every such aspersions or judgments,
bowing my head to graciously
to thank my Maker who made no mistake
in creating me an African
and in His wonderful image.

You Grew Taller Than the Palm

I saw the blade that broke
through the hard shell
push through the surrounding ashes
of the African soil and begin to rise.
It caught my attention.

There, in the sun, in the rain,
in the dust, she stood,
refusing to buckle under pressure.

As days went by
the wind came again and again,
gnawing the ball of the little coconut palm,
until it left bite marks
on her slender stem.

With each new bite
and each new lash
each new day
the little palm stretched
and stretched in pain.

With each new gouge
and each new scar
the little palm stretched

Ikechi Akurunwa

and stretched in pain,
day after day,
until it stretched
and stretched
to a great height, becoming
the first thing I notice
every time
I open my back door.

Madiba, the great African Madiba,
you grew taller than the palm.
You erased your pain
with your great height.
You erased your shame
with a statue no one can ignore.

Standing taller than the palm,
you withstood the winds
of strife and humiliation
with the heart of a warrior.

Standing taller than the palm
you withstood the lashes of hatred
that tried to break your unyielding
African spirit, shrugging off
the spite and torturing
arrows of racism
with your mortified skin.

You Grew Taller Than The Palm

Madiba, the great African Madiba,
rising above the dust of Apartheid,
you grew taller than the palm.

Yes, you did.

Ikechi Akurunwa

You Grew Taller Than The Palm

TWO

The sound of the groaning and gnashing of teeth
in the land of Africa
is loud enough for every ear to hear
but many pretend
they do not hear it.

Ikechi Akurunwa

I Have Seen So Much

Some days, I am miserable,
drowning in the anguish
surging in my mind
like galloping waves
until my soul is nudged
by the invisible hand of hope
to rise for the journey ahead.

We are many on this miserable walk;
the impoverished offspring of Africa,
wrestling with the strangling hands
of oppression and hardship on our necks.

Many have died in their suffering,
but many are still forging ahead with me.
We know ourselves
and can identify each other from afar.
Even the soles of our tired feet
leave similar marks on the ground
as we sway down the road with our burdens.

And because we have become comrades
in our hydra headed struggles, each time
I walk from one African village to another
many see me as a friend, a brother, a kinsman,

sometimes grinning at me,
sometimes waving with hands hanging
from their shoulders
by thin, threadbare muscles.

They have beautiful names,
but their pains are deep and ugly.
The murmurs from their huts
buried deep
in the dark shadow of poverty
haunt me every day.

Oh, I have seen so much pain in these villages,
so much anguish from their frightened faces.
I have seen too many children with marasmus,
too many young mothers looking like old rags.
I have heard too many men curse
the day they were born,
and too many teenagers
wishing they were never born.

And because of the misery pulling them
with long and tangled leashes
through dark and smoldering dawns,
I walk daily through this miserable land of Africa
digging for the hidden balm or poultice
that can heal their pain and mine.

Sometimes the weight of it all drives me

to clutch my weeping pen like a gat,
squeezing it hard until teary poems
flow from my wounded heart.

And because their eyes and mine have seen
so many promising rains
come and go
without washing away the footprints
of poverty from our soil,

and because their ears and mine have heard
the sound of so many promising winds
come and go
without erasing the marks and furrows
of poverty from our land,

I will continue to tell their stories and mine
until the waves of exploitation and repression,
drowning our land in the deep sea
of hardship and untenable poverty,
end their relentless siege.

Ikechi Akurunwa

Wooden Treasure

I know the smell of fresh woods.
It's not hidden from anyone
like the tiny eyes
of grandma's Christmas mittens.

I know the smell of fresh woods
like the smell of her new mittens
and I carve them into relics
of sweet and bitter memories
with the tip of my pen,
one stroke at a time,
the same way grandma weaves
her mittens, one thread at a time,
for the sweet memories of Christmas.

I know I come from the dust,
from roots shriveled by the tropical sun,
from a lineage with no royal crown
or castle towering on the hill,

but I come from parents
who spared nothing for me,
parents who made light of life
with their infectious smiles,
a mother whose heart

bleeds every day for the poor,
and a father whose hands always
had the scalpel to debride until it heals
the wound on the skin of human conscience.

Sometimes I am mistaken as a blind deer
because I come from a village slowly emerging
from the shadows of the gravestones
of ancient cultures and traditions,
and a tribe that is an island lost on the map
like a mythical star, yet undeniably
existing in the unseen galaxies of the world
like lost ancient gemstones gleaming
from sea-beds and lighting
the dark sky above.

At other times, I am mistaken as an ocean
because I come from a nation
howling daily
like an angry sea, like a caged octopus
thrashing in the sun; a nation
whose crown is so fractured
it can only fit on the wrong head.

And because of her screams
and her painful stings,
my face has been scarred
like a mask.

Ikechi Akurunwa

But that has not robbed me
of my love for the woods.
I still cherish their secret powers.
I still love to sleep and wake up
in their strong arms
or sit under their canopies
to engrave my weeping poems
in the furrows of their palm.

And until the African sky is bright again,
until our streets are safe again
to walk with our children,
until truth becomes the air we breathe,
and words regain their true meaning,
I will continue to carve the bark of trees,
burying in their secret vaults, for posterity,
every virtue I can glean from the dying
memories of our centenarians,
and from the sacrosanct warnings
of the few angels still walking the earth.

And for those who cannot wait for the odious
and ominous future to slowly unfold,
for your sake and as a testament
that a certain poet who passed
through this hemisphere
did not shy away
from telling the truth,
I will always carve the bark of trees

and boldly engrave a warning on them,
every time I see an evil cloud
looming in our sky.

We have come a long way together,
the woods and I. That is why
they always hear my voice
and solemn whispers.

Every day, they spread the tears
dripping from the mouth of my pen
like grains falling to the ground.

Ikechi Akurunwa

A Forgotten People

When the exuberant African morning came
unwrapping its gift to me,
a gentle and friendly wind came with it,
pouring through the window vents
of my village house and waking up
the old rivers of love for the tropics
sleeping in my veins.

And when shortly after the tropical sun
fully emerged in its glory and grandeur,
the heart of the whole village grew warm.
And everywhere I turned, my ears were filled
with the forgotten voices of village life—

the voices of women going to the market
to buy or sell,

the voices of palm wine lovers
haggling prices with palm wine tappers
carrying effervescing kegs of fresh wine,

the voices of men rushing to the bush
to check their traps for bushmeat,

the voices of farmers

You Grew Taller Than The Palm

going to their farms to begin
the arduous task of preparing
their farmlands for the planting season.

Echoes of joy and jubilation
resonated from every corner—

from elders in colorful hats
whistling with their mouths
to convey secrets to each other
as they passed by,

from teenage boys
nosing around girls craving
and demanding attention.

But when after sunset, the mad flood
of the tropical darkness rushed in
and the whole village quickly died,
my heart sank from seeing with the misery
the darkness brought to a village
with hardly any electricity.

I went to bed wondering how many people
would wake up in the morning
with their mind still sound and sane.

And as the village laid bare in the dark,
I strained my ears for any sign of life

from the villagers trying to sleep,
wrapped in their old tattered sheets
of poverty and hardship,
in their dark huts
like mummies.

It was a painful and sleepless night,
after a long absence from my village.
It was the night I heard the loudest cries
of my forgotten and forsaken village.
It was the night the pain in their hearts
rang a loud bell in my ears
until I heard
all the silent murmurs,
all the silent groans,
all the silent tears,
they silently heaped
on their deaf pillows.

It was as if, before dawn, the rotten
and nauseating smell of poverty
suppressed for years by the unyielding
spirit of the villagers blew its lid in my face,
heaping on me the burden of guilt
too heavy to bear.

Since then, I have been haunted
by the scowling sound of death
I heard that night pounding

constantly on their doors,

and by the thought of the enormous burdens
they drag along each day
that will never be heard on the news,
in a country where people die in silence.

Ikechi Akurunwa

Not Enough Time

Why does the day swell like a whirling wind
each time people gather to hear my story,
distracting their itching ears?

Why does it take off in hysteria
like a frightened bird flying blindly
towards the growing shadow of twilight
each time the silvery ray of hope
trembling in my heart
begins to bloom?

Why does it draw down its curtain
and turn off the lights in a hurry
when it hears my voice
discharging like a broken bell
the sorrows of Africa
on the silent ears of the world?

Is the day a blind guide?
Another servant the night delegates
to finish its unfinished business?

I am appalled by the brute force
with which darkness reclaims
the land from the hand of the day.

You Grew Taller Than The Palm

And because there is not enough time
for me to tell the stories of all the pains
and the agonies of Africans
to anyone who will listen;
I am sometimes frustrated that the day
does not utter a word of explanation
to anyone
for failing to restrain
the intrusive hands of the night
as they exchange their duty posts.

Ikechi Akurunwa

If You Are Looking for Me

If you are looking for another poor fellow
bearing a burden as heavy as yours,
then you have found a compatriot
not deterred by the stench of digging
through the old ruins of Africa
for a grain of silvery hope
for the dying Africans.

But if you are looking for someone
to tell you the same old fairytales
Africans have been fed for ages,
I have no such fables to offer.

And after you have wandered through the day
watching hills with domes I didn't build,
admiring the golden statues of our monarchs,
and dreaming of becoming a big political bigwig,
if you decide to look for me,
there, in those scrambled letters of my poetry,
you will see my face.

And after you have hobnobbed
with some of those African millionaires
who never worked for their millions,
and politicians who never earned their votes,

You Grew Taller Than The Palm

if you decide to look for me,
there, in those alphabets
dripping from my pen like bile,
you will hear my heartbeat.

And after you have knocked
on the endless stream of houses
glowing like bioluminescent waves,
and have been snubbed by their opulent occupants
who don't care about your pain or mine,
if you decide to look for me,
come to the nests without colored feathers,

and there, in those hollowed-out places
where my words will not matter
except to Africans rebuilding their broken walls,
you will find me.

And after you have been drawn
to one of those theaters
where singers endlessly praise men
with many lofty crowns and mantles,
men who can change the tide of a nation's politics
with one wave of their hand,
if you decide to look for me,
search for me in those places
with broken chairs and tables
that still offer half of their legs
to me to sit

as I write or speak
without applause or attention
except the silent nudge
from those forbidden to utter a word
about their burned down
African dreams.

And at the end of the day,
if you become tired of looking
for one of your imagined gods
who will grant you all your wishes,
if you decide to look for me, look in
those pigmented alphabets of my poems
pouring like rain from my hand,
or look on those trees bearing
my flowering verses as fruits,
watered by my tears.

And until you draw your bias curtain
and look closely at the tears of joy
and the tears of sadness
dripping from my verses,
you will still be looking for me.

Come with Me

With the limbs of the African dawn
bitten off by the rabid mouth of poverty
and paraded daily as a trophy
by the teeth and claws of greed,
how can I hold my silence?

How can I hold my silence
when I've lost count of the graves
of children whose lights were too quickly
extinguished on the candelabras they held up
to salute the land of their birth;

children who were not allowed to plant
deep roots in the impervious African soil
before they were overrun by the waves
of the seas inflamed with rage?

Shake off your amnesia and draw close.
I have not come with a sword
or an emissary note from the West,
but as a brother, a father,
a heartbroken African.

I have come to weep for children
that have exhausted their tears,

children whose hearts are full of fears
as they stare blankly
at their vanishing dreams.

Shake off your apathy
and come with me. Come,
let us exert every tenable force
until we wake up the dying cinders
of our land with the echoes
of the hushed vines
of our children.

Come, let us drum on every
cymbal of hope in our land
until the drowned voices
of our children are awakened.
Let us plead their cases
before kings and princes,
before noble and honorable men,
until our pleas fall
like seeds and sprout.

Until our children are happy
and proud to be Africans,
smiling, singing, and laughing together
like clusters of roses
blazing with hope,
our job is not done.

You Grew Taller Than The Palm

Until then, come with me, my friend;
see what I am seeing,
feel what I am feeling.

You have been silent for too long!

Ikechi Akurunwa

All Is Not Well

The strange sounds in the air
have thrown the whole land into fear.
The insidious red magma
of greed and corruption
that has been belching and convulsing
in the dark heart of our land for years
has erupted, and now the land
is regurgitating all the evil
it was fed.

Death, with its dark sickle,
is waiting at every gate
in our land
for blind and wandering feet.

All our byways have been overrun
by strange thorns, flung like spears
by the vengeful wind
of the betrayed African dawn.

All is not well, my brother.
All is not well, my sister.
Even the old faithful moon
has retreated from our hills.
The stars are beginning to flee

from our nests. And soon,
our skyline will be left to sob
on the shoulders of dark mountains.

We have become a vulnerable people —
a people gripped daily by the fear
of the looming shadow of imminent doom
and we can't go on pretending,
day after day that all is well.

All is not well, my brother.
All is not well, my sister.
All is not well.

Ikechi Akurunwa

A Strong Resolve

I don't pick fights on rainy days,
but this drizzling, murmuring rain,
falling from the eyes of Africans
because of the darkening cloud of subjugation,
will not dampen my resolve today
to sound an alarm.

With the fire of optimism waning
and the spirit of despair rising,
with the bell of hope slowly dying
and the untamed gouges of hunger
daily wearing out the patience of our children,
I have come to sound a desperate alarm
in the ears of the elders of our land,

elders still silently staring
at the tortured shadow
of our tumbling ground
while our youth are fleeing
across the Atlantic to foreign lands
in search of a better life.

With no more graves to bury the dead,
with no more words to soothe the pain
of fathers and mothers who stare daily

through their silent windows for answers
I have come to sound a desperate alarm
in the stuffed ears of our politicians
hypnotized by the glitz and glamor
of pleasure and unmitigated power.

And because nothing can better convey
the urgency of my message,
I will continue to sound the alarm
with unwavering determination,
even with heavy eyelids and a body
worn out from the exhaustion of seeing
the disintegrating parts of Africa
falling like dead wood into ready coffins
carved by the hands of those that profit
from the slew of Africa's woes.

Even without the blessings of great oratory
and the fragrance of fame and fortune,
I will continue to sound the alarm
until the day all Africans
wipe the tears of years
of painful subjugation
from their eyes
to see the light of a new dawn
getting brighter and brighter
like the mast of a lost ship, slowly rising
from the belly of the dark ocean.

Ikechi Akurunwa

The Dancing Feather

It was as if they emerged with the eerie morning,
those who know me and those who do not,
racing down to bear witness against me
for crying in the open for Africa.

It is an unseasonable time in Africa.
The truth has become a taboo,
a heavy cross to bear.

I blew the forbidden trumpet,
waking up all the political zealots and stooges,
a vicious army
ready to die defending
the steady flow of their filthy lucre,
traitors who have scared angels away
from our streets, churches,
and government.

With flaming arrogance and audacity
they drummed into my ears
threats of my coming doom
until they drained
their voice and mine.
But my silenced words
continued to burn in my heart

You Grew Taller Than The Palm

like an ember that refused to die.

And because of them,
everyone abhorred my sight,
staring at me from a distance
with eyes dilated by fear,
until something beckoned me
from the sky.

It was a lonely feather,
a lonely, beautiful feather,
dancing at the nudge of the wind,
fluttering in the air
like a happy little bird.

As I watched it float
and dance effortlessly,
with no signs of worry
or sadness,
something about it
excited me.

And the more it waved
its billowing barbs and barbules,
the more I got excited.

At the backdrop of a white sky
it looked like a white dove
wrapped

Ikechi Akurunwa

in the little body of a feather,
with wings choreographed
with grace and candor.

I was engrossed in this mount
of transfiguration experience
until my heart was flooded with boundless joy,
making the weight of the bestial day
weightless on my shoulder,
as weightless as the little feather
dancing for me.

With a feeling of exhilaration,
I waved at my little companion,
oblivious of the world around me
until it vanished from my teary eyes.

And as I wiped my eyes,
I became convinced
this was a sign from heaven
to never stop fighting
until the dead conscience
of Africa
is awakened.

Oh, Come Rain

When will the gods of this land
relent from goading the African sky
with their ironclad horns
so that a good, unfettered rain can fall
on the thirsty and parched acres
of my tongue?

Oh, come sweet rain, come.
Oh, come meticulous drummer,
seasoned piper, the mirror
I look into and see rainbows
and stars all around me,
the world I roam unreservedly
with scars and tears no one can see,
the wall I walk through effortlessly,
greeted by thunderous cheers.

Oh, come sweet rain, come.
Oh, come anointed orchestra.
Come and cast your crystal beads in the air
and let them chant in my ears
until my joy peaks
like the crescendo
of crystal harps,
oblivious of the noise around.

Ikechi Akurunwa

I am tired of hearing the sound
of guns from meaningless wars.
I am tired of hearing racial bells
deliberately rung in my ears
all day and all night.
I am tired of hearing the vain words
of mortals who bend their mouths
like crooked bows to brag about the hair
on their brow or the color of the skin
they had no part in creating
or choosing for themselves.

Oh, come sweet rain, come.
Oh, come symphony of a thousand voices.
Come and purge the air of the noise
from the callous mouth of the world.
I am tired of hearing the dubious voices
of politicians looking for someone
to sell their newly baked lies to.
I am tired of hearing tyrants pounding
their feet like gods and threatening
to call down fire from heaven.
I am tired of hearing despots,
forcing themselves into power
and days later boasting
as arbiters of justice.

Oh, come sweet rain, come.
You are the music my soul longs for,

You Grew Taller Than The Palm

the only melody that can soothe
the anguish of my tortured ears.

Ikechi Akurunwa

THREE

Oh Africa, your children are falling
at the hands of each other.
It's an anathema!

Ikechi Akurunwa

What Troubles Me

It's not the callousness or the craftiness
of the passing wind that time and again
tries to unveil the hidden scars
on the face of my village
that bothers me.

It's not even the attention-seeking
tetchy crickets and mosquitoes
feeding my insomnia every night
that preoccupy my mind.
They have been kinder to me and my village
than the endless generations of African
authoritarians ruling with iron hands.

I have been startled a few times
by the pilfering hands of senility,
how every day
it secretly and quietly
steals the glare on the face,
but I do not lose sleep over it,
or over the stubborn weed of poverty
that I have not been able to completely
uproot from my life or village.
They have been kinder to me and my village
than the mocking voices of the lords of our land

as they impose themselves over us day after day.

The eyes that have not bled
have not seen what I have seen
in the villages and cities of Africa:
farmlands turned into wastelands,
shadows of battered shores and looted barns
littered like ruins of war,
like ghost towns and cities
overrun by sandstorms.

I have always wondered
which hand beats this wild drum of greed,
which bird sings this hypnotizing song of avarice
in the ears of African politicians?
Their quest for fame and fortune,
their insatiable craving for power,
their lust for unfathomed pleasure and leisure,
their unholy alliance with evil,
have ceaselessly invited twisted days
and long grueling nights of shame and pain,
faceless and mocking clouds
splattering poverty and misery
on the faces of Africans.
As if this is the badge of honor
all Africans must wear
or die.

With nothing left in our land

You Grew Taller Than The Palm

but little flickers of dying light,
and the ruin and wreckage
of years of bad governance,
this saddle, this steel saddle
of subjugation around our necks,
like the yoke of oxen,
will one day crush us
to death
if we continue
to bear it
in silence.

Ikechi Akurunwa

Letter to the Black African President

i
Your Excellency,
how does this broken system
of a broken system
of a broken system
of a broken system
you feel so entitled to,
not bother you
from day to day?

Your Excellency,
how does this broken system
of a broken system
of a broken system
of a broken system
you have continued to break
into more pieces
not bother you
from year to year?

ii
Your Excellency,
Mr. President —

fathers have died,
mothers have died,
children have died,
all in your hands.

Villages have died,
towns have died,
cities have died,
all in your hands.

Mills have died,
factories have died,
industries have died,
all in your hands.

Dreams have died,
hopes have died,
aspirations have died,
all in your hands.

Peace has died,
laughter has died,
trust has died,
all in your hands.

Everything great has died,
everything small has died,
everything beautiful has died,
all in your hands.

iii
Your Excellency, perhaps
I am missing something.

Please, tell me,
how this leprous land
and the rusty chains of suppression
cutting our flesh day and night,
fail to rouse your soul to sympathy?

Your Excellency,
as a follow-up question,
please, tell me,
how are you able to feign blindness
to these piles of broken walls
and stacks of emptied and broken coffers?

How does the sordid scene
of caged, frothing, and cachexic prisoners
being slowly starved to death
not sicken you or awaken
your dead conscience?

One final question, Your Excellency.
Please, sir, tell me,
how does it not bother you
that birds sing all day in our land,

jumping happily from one tree to the other,
but little children can't
because of the pangs of hunger?

How does it not bother you
that flowers smile all day in our land,
but little children can't
because of the gloom
written
all over the faces of their parents
finding it hard to fend for them?

Sorry, Your Excellency,
just one more question!
Please, tell me, sir,
how does it not bother you
that while our land has been reduced
to a pile of rubble like an old abandoned mine,
you still happily place the little we have left
in the full hands of our colonial masters,
at any little nudge?

Is that how our moribund land,
with seething anger and unbridled anguish,
will rise from its ashes?

Your Excellency, perhaps,
I am really, really
missing something.

Ikechi Akurunwa

Poor Historian

The African soil knows the pain
of bearing the huge weight of dictators,
whose iron feet are always aimed
at the fragile backs of defenseless Africans,
ready to squash them like bugs
if they dare demand the right to be heard.

It is a burden we bear in silence,
a cross we carry each day
like beasts of burden.
Many generations have passed
through this treacherous flame
with wounds too deep to heal.

Sometimes our tears become the river
we use to wash the feet of one another
as we huddle together night and day,
afraid of their hatchets,
afraid of their guns,
afraid of their claws,
afraid of their gallows,
afraid of their submerged prisons
where no one leaves alive.

Oh, poor historian, the husky tree that loves

You Grew Taller Than The Palm

to bask alone in the African sun,
ask the Acacia tree that lost
all her leaves and boughs
in one storm,
what happened?

But I know you will not ask.
I know you will cling to power
until the strong hands of retribution or death
snatches it away from your grip.

Ikechi Akurunwa

Devoured Inheritance

Lately, all I do in my dreams
is scuttle or huddle with my shadow
as I try to straighten the wrinkled face of Africa,
strewing letters like a powdery poultice
on our crusted wounds.

Some nights my mind excitedly sails with the moon
until the dawn of a new day,
but begins to bleed once I behold the sight
of our remaining pastures and granaries
being washed ashore
by the venting storms of dead rivers,
angered by the iron wings of brigands
who have gutted our coffers
and are still asking for more.

Every day, their scorching footprints
rip through our land like wildfire,
leaving behind death and desolation.

With their rods, they have pitted
fathers against sons,
daughters against mothers.

They have perfected the act of stuffing

the mouths of the gullible with cheap candies
until they turn each one of them into zealots
bearing spears and arrows for them.

But we cannot continue to watch our land die
or be dragged along this destructive path
by overzealous autocrats
while we stare from afar
or through a veiled window,

else their talons will sharpen more and more,
making them more vicious and powerful villains
and making us frightened and vulnerable prey.

Ikechi Akurunwa

Heart Cry from the Slum

Out there, where we live, the only pod
left on the tree is the putrid pod.
The only flame burning at night
is the glow of a cigarette dangling
from the mouth of a lonely man.

Out there, where we live,
everything sacred or of value
has been splintered like deadwood
by the axes of those who profit
from the misfortunes of the poor.

Out there, where we live,
the groaning of trampled dreams
constantly quivers under our feet.
And the church, our only solace,
vibrates daily with the aching voices
of praying Christians who, long ago,
realized that our enemies
are stronger than we are.

But while we wait
for Archangel Gabriel or Michael
to come and deliver us,
I have vowed that from this slum

You Grew Taller Than The Palm

where poverty seeps from every crevice,
I will fight day and night
until we hear the sound of honor,
and joy rises from our parched land
like a fountain, erasing the smears
and jeers of shame we have borne
like a curse for many long years.

For all those tired of singing dirges all night,
and reciting sorrowful rhymes to their children,
this is time to come together
to fight for our dignity and freedom,
else the whirling dust
from the trampling feet of subjugation,
will bury us in an unmarked grave,

as if we never existed,
as if we never tried,
as if we were not worthy
to advance the course of humanity,
or leave our mark on this earth.

Ikechi Akurunwa

How Did You Forget?

I will not forget those days you came
wielding in our faces
hands that devour like wildfire
hands that roar like thunder
hands that crush like a sledgehammer.

I will not forget those days you came
striking like a plague,
biting like a python,
stinging like a scorpion,
ruining our lives and dreams
time and time again.

Because of your incessant terror,
the night constantly hummed and drummed
the music of death that made even the brave
tread lightly on the ground,
constantly looking back over their shoulders
as they weaved their broken dreams
together, again and again.

Because of your terror,
our mouths could not speak
what our eyes saw.
Our jittery lips could not say

You Grew Taller Than The Palm

what our ears heard.
Only our sad and tired faces,
our bleeding wounds,
our eyes full of tears
told the stories of our torture
to our children and the blind world.

Then one day, one ordinary day,
our years of pain and heartaches,
our years of groaning and moaning,
our years of sadness and sorrows
drove the hand of justice
to shake the land while we slept.

We woke to find your throne had fallen
and your footprints had been washed away
by the rain of equity and justice.

It was like a dream
in which all our scars vanished.

When we had no more desire to live,
we awoke to a new dawn.
When we had no more wish for glamor,
we woke up to the glare of a glorious sky.
When we had no more eagerness to sing,
or an ear willing to entertain music,
we woke up to a chorus of birds.

Ikechi Akurunwa

It was a new day, an unambiguous day,
a day we never thought we would see.
When our hearts no longer
felt the nudge of hope,
hope came knocking on our door.
When our souls had become a dry
and barren land,
the hand of mercy came
offering us rest and peace.

It was a day of judgment.
The day death came,
not for one of us
praying for it,
but for the tyrant, the seemingly
invincible tyrant,

striking him so hard
that it silenced him forever.

Oh tyrant, tyrant, tyrant,
the wicked and impossible tyrant,
the fire-spitting god
that must be appeased
and worshipped, day and night.
How did you forget you were mortal?
How did you forget
you will not live forever?
How did you forget?

You Grew Taller Than The Palm

How did you forget?

Ikechi Akurunwa

This Land

Misery flying like harmattan dust
has perfected its flight and the act
of building
gray tombs
on the faces and hair of the poor
dragging their tired feet every day
along dusty streets of Africa,
begging for bread.

The endless wind of tyranny
has turned our fertile lands
into wastelands,
into seas of dusty mounds,
into graveyards of looted galleries,
into relics of empty wells
and gutted coffers.

This land, this looted land of Africa,
where ripples of laughter are no longer heard,
where duet singing robins
have been chased away
with the stone of avarice;
if it could mount a defense,
would absolve itself
from the blood of the poor

You Grew Taller Than The Palm

left to die of hunger
each day
in grimy streets and fields
where vultures come to feast.

This land, this plundered land of Africa,
where dancing stars no longer appear in the sky,
where town criers and clerics
are tired of announcing burials;
if it could speak, it would thunder
all day and all night,
in uncontrollable rage,
until we come together to rebuild
its broken walls and hedges.

And surely, this land,
this pillaged land of Africa,
drenched with the blood
of the poor and the innocent,
one day, will speak.

Against All Odds

Africa, the ancient
cradle of the human race
the tree with interminable roots
the golden vine that the prying hands
of the world has given no rest,
is today shivering like a child
gripped with fear.

The remnants of a crooked era
claw through her soul
like a grieving mother.

Sometimes, I see her walking, half dead.
Sometimes, I see her limping, half dead
the grimace on her face as disturbing
as a brawling night.

And sometimes, I see her high spirited,
looking invincible and forging ahead,
against all odds, like someone not afraid
of the burdens on her shoulders
or the death chasing her.

Perhaps, time is a villain and a friend.
Perhaps we have crossed a line

our forefathers didn't cross.
Perhaps we have bitten the finger of God.
I don't know.

But I never thought in my lifetime
I would see rivers hardening like rocks
around the feet of our children
or carpenter ants burrowing into our flesh
to build their ugly nests.

I never thought in my lifetime
I would see our farmlands
turned into graveyards,
or the hands of greed and corruption
splitting our kingdom into warring
and irreparable factions.

From coast to coast, by day and by night,
the dark sea of tyranny looms
like a treacherous storm, leaving
the air tense with fear and anger.

But no matter how bleak
the journey becomes,
no matter what turn it takes
as the oppressors tighten their grip,
we will remain strong,
not recounting our misfortunes
or shedding tears of self-pity,

for the journey is still far and long.

And if someday, we reach the shores
of a new dawn,
there, in the open, before every eye,
I will sing for Africa.
I will cheer and tell her
the brave stories of her children.
I will tell her of our constant drumbeat
of hope in the face of hardship,
our refusal to kiss the sugar-coated
lips of politicians, or shake
their blood-stained hands.

Whenever we set our feet
on the hallowed ground of freedom—
if we ever do—
on that faithful day I hope and pray to see,
I will dance and dance
all day and all night,
till our wounds heal,
and our joy returns.

FOUR

Africa's greatest weakness
is her kind heart.

Ikechi Akurunwa

Self-Destruction

Everywhere I go I see the tree
bowing to the wind and to the world
like someone under a spell,
someone willing to bow day and night
to appease herself or someone else,
even if she grows a hunchback,
or loses all her Medusa's hair to the wind.

Maybe, she ought to ask Africa
what she gained bowing for centuries
to Europe and the rest of the world.

All bowing did
was to turn Africa
into a foot-mart,
a vulnerable prey,
a hutch left to slowly die
a shameful and lonely death.

And if you look closely at her,
you will see a famished soul,
a continent reduced to a leaf
sulking in the air like twilight,
a shadow frittering like cold ashes,
a fallen tree rotting away in the sand,

a gutted shell howling daily in the wind
to the deaf ears of the world.

Dangerous Trend

Oh time, the thread that weaves years together
until they become a colossal sea.
The hand that stretches a day and its dreams
into a deep, dark chasm,
the ancient captain of the boat
that cannot be moored,
row, row,
row back your boat,
bring back the good old days
you hauled away.

Oh time, swing, swing,
swing back your pendulum
to those hallowed days
when the strongest and wisest men
in the world
were Africans.
When the richest merchants
in the world
were Africans
and Africa was to the world a galaxy
with the pure aroma
of heaven.

Oh time, what did you do to the African man?

Ikechi Akurunwa

It seems after crossing many time zones,
the African man lost everything
he gained while he charted the course
of his life and continent.

Oh time, what did you do to the African man?
He seems to have lost his bearing
after he was thrust into a world
with too many blind alleys.

Oh time, what did you do to the African man?
It seems after he was invaded
from the Western frontiers
by those who mispronounced his name
he began to mispronounce his own name
until he lost his identity.

From this high pedestal of illusions,
from this exalted altar of false alternatives,
from this sea of misguiding jingles,
he seems to be metamorphosing
into a brittle ribbon
a fragile statue
a stagnant river.

And without imminent intervention,
the deceptive hands of ease and comfort,
the devouring mouth of new age
will consume the last ounce of his dignity

and tear down the last walls
of his moral and ethical boundaries.

Ikechi Akurunwa

The African Heart

Africa, from the angry Sahara Desert,
from the dividing lines of the equator,
from the greedy hands of the seas,
you gathered your fifty-five children
into one enviable family.

Then the Sahara dust came and you survived,
the harmattan wind came and you survived,
the mosquitoes came and you survived,
but when the West came
your nightmare began.

I cannot understand the African heart.
With only a few petulant knocks,
you threw your door wide open
and let in chameleons with hidden guns.
At the time you still ruled
your kingdom like a deity.

I cannot understand the African heart.
With one false promise from outlaws,
you allowed yourself to be raided
and traded for guns and mortars
that are now killing your children.
At the time you still charted

the course of your destiny.

I cannot understand the African heart.
With only a few sermons
from sacrilegious priests,
you allowed yourself
to be gathered into sacks
and sold like cheap merchandise
on Western auction blocks.
At a time when you still wielded
power and authority.

But despite all you have been through,
nothing steals your joy
or dampens your spirit. Even when
the voice of the day rises and falls
like the voice of roaring thunder,
you still find a way to nudge your tongue
to sing and rouse
everyone around
to sing with you.

Ah, Africa, without a doubt
or hedging of the truth, there are things
that won't change with you:
your warm and kind hear,
your sweet and genuine smile,
your fervent and enduring love

but you are paying a steep price,
a very steep price,
for your enduring virtues.

Bundles of Nothing

Of a certainty, the wind can build castles
from mere rubble and bobbles,
gluing them together like girdles
with a thread that twiddles.

Of a certainty, the wind is restless.
At sundown or sunrise
it gathers bits and pieces
of objects with surfaces that glaze or crease,
working with the wisdom of a sage
to create a maze
that stuns the mind and the eyes.

Of a certainty, as the day glides,
shuffling its shadows like bands
of happy, ubiquitous birds,
the wind can pace by leaps and bounds,
in low and high grounds,
with rakes in her hands.

Gathering and hauling weeds and fronds
until her rising castles of litter and sod
turn flourishing farmlands
and green and trim yards
into wastelands.

Ikechi Akurunwa

Of a certainty, dreams
can be built from the scratch,
but not with those empty straws
or bundles of hollow stalks
that quickly rot in the sand.

Invitation

In luminescent syllables
the tropical day babbles,
wide awake before dawn's garbles
and the usual street squabbles.

Over the sprawling African hills
the aura of the rising sun kindles
a fire of hope that marvels and dazzles
even the hermits and lazybones.

And as time races through the maze
and daze of the sun's rays,
ambitious people competing in every race
surge through the air, land, and sea

reaching for every ounce of treasure
and every bite of pleasure
until the sun lumbers across the roof with leisure,
hugging everyone without measure.

And when caught in this rat race
I stop to wonder if the endowment of time,
the daily rush to keep up with time,
is a leash I must fight with every minute.

Ikechi Akurunwa

Or is it a summon,
a unique invitation at dawn
to make a worthy mark before the curtain
of the day is drawn?

Little by Little

There exists every day,
inside my skull,
a volley of tortured thoughts,

thoughts whirling in my brain
over Africa's bones, rotten like fish,
over her hair, bristled or greyed by grief,
over her flesh
daily being devoured
by the fiery lips of greed.

These thoughts race inside
my doorless skull
day after day,
heaping on my neck a weight
as heavy as the burden
in the heart of a poet
bearing the guilt
of an untold story.

That's why I live towing,
with other benevolent Africans,
the trail of the flames
consuming the land of Africa,
laboring to rescue what I can,

no matter how small;

knowing that little by little,
we can take back Africa,
and change
the direction she is heading.

You Grew Taller Than The Palm

My Afro-Caribbean Brothers and Sisters

Your islands studded
in the cleft of eclectic hills
like precious stones gleaming
in the bowl of a diamond
are the reason the world cannot resist
coming to see how heaven lays
golden eggs in your evening skies,
cheered by the thunderous voices
of your blue oceans and the waving hands
of your exuberant palm trees.

We love to brag about you in Africa
because no one can imitate the smiles
you inherited from our genial bloodline
or replicate the laughter
we put in your mouth
that rings like the church bell
gathering people to your sacred shores
from all over the world to adore
the handiworks of God
with a merry heart.

And no matter who comes
to your dreamland
to laugh and dance with you,

Ikechi Akurunwa

no one can match
those dancing steps we gave you,
those African vines
flowering all over you
with roots that cannot wither.

So, as the world courts you,
wining and dining with you,
and taking a piece of you home as a souvenir,
do not forget there is a piece of you in me,
and a piece of me in you.
Do not forget we are brothers and sisters.
Our paths will always cross.

I Still Believe

Over the years, time, like the wind
has combed through the universe of my head,
degrading its landscape with senile tremors
until most of its valuable assets
greyed and died,
and now there are things I may never
decipher or remember again.

I may never know why
there are no more rainbows
in the African sky to grab the attention
of children in the village
and distract them for a while
from the gripping pains of hunger.

I may never know why
there are no more happy stars and moons
guiding youth in the village
through the thick African darkness
to the river to fetch water
so they won't stub their toes
on hard objects and fall,
spilling the water
they walked miles to fetch.

Ikechi Akurunwa

I may never know why there are no more
silvery rains splattering on the ground,
nibbling the feet of village children
to excite them for a while and distract them
from the endless requiems of man after man,
woman after woman, child after child,
dropping dead every day
from the perennial plagues
of drought and hardship
in the village.

I may never know why some creatures
wear the night as a garment
while the tropical sun is blazing
or why lions are crowned
the king of the jungle
where there is an abundance
of elephants and giraffes.

And I may never know why,
when it was my turn to be crowned an elder,
the once cherished and adored honor
bestowed on every grey-haired African,
became a thing of the past.
I lost a title that would have qualified me
as a man full of ancient wisdom,
a man age has gifted
with rare proverbs and idioms
and can easily draw a large crowd of admirers

once he opens his mouth to speak.

Who would have thought
that such a galvanizing
ancient tradition handed down
to us by our forefathers,
would one day be discarded
like an old rag.

A lot has changed,
indeed, a lot has changed.
I no longer recognize the face of Africa:
her lips maligned by pain and suffering,
her eyes worn by long nights of grief,
her cheeks drained of every color
by the wringing hands of perennial
subjugation and exploitation.

But I still believe in Africa,
I will always believe
that Africa is the citrine stone
with a fire no one can quench.

And I will keep on believing
that one day, our children
will rise
to restore
the lost glory
of Africa.

Ikechi Akurunwa

Sound the Alarm

Friend, I have wept
for things
you know about
and things you don't.

I have swum in seas without water,
and waters without seas and shorelines
looking for the last ship that carted away
the African fortune.

I have climbed walls and hills
with ivies, soldier ants, geckos, and snakes,
sniffing for the last whiff of the black smoke
that blinded the eyes of the African dawn.

If the truth be told, I have parted
the curtain wide enough for you to see
the growing dark cloud
in the African sky.

And at this hour I leave you
to sound the alarm with me
with the trumpet I've placed in your hand,
or go back to sleep.

www.ingramcontent.com/pod-product-compliance
Lightning Source LLC
Chambersburg PA
CBHW031558040426
42452CB00006B/339